TRAVELLING INWARDS

St Teresa's *Interior Castle* for Everyone

For all those who have been
my mothers, sisters and companions
in the religious life

TRAVELLING INWARDS

St Teresa's *Interior Castle* for Everyone

Simplified and illustrated by
Elizabeth Ruth Obbard

New City

First published in 2013
in Great Britain by
New City

© 2013 Elizabeth Ruth Obbard
2017 second reprint
2019 third reprint

Graphics and cover design by Hildebrando Moguiê

British Cataloguing-in-Publication Data:
A catalogue record for this book is available from
the British Library
ISBN 978-1-905039-21-4

Typeset in Great Britain by
New City, London

Printed and bound by Books Factory

CONTENTS

Introduction 7

The Interior Castle 17

Preface 19
Mansion 1 21
   The image of the castle 21
   The reality of sin 23
   The palmito 24
   The bee in the honeycomb 25
   Giving time to prayer 26
Mansion 2 29
   How God speaks to us in the second mansion 29
   Feelings and favours 31
   True peace 31

Mansion 3 35
   Qualities of the third mansion 35
   On being tested 37
   Doing penance 39
   Look to your own failings 40

Mansion 4 43
   Nearer to the King 43
   Sweetness in prayer and spiritual consolations 43
   Distracting thoughts 44
   The Prayer of Quiet 46
   The Prayer of Recollection 47
   Awakening love 49
   Two warnings 50

Mansion 5 53
   The analogy of the silkworm 53
   The soul as a wax seal 56
   The importance of loving others 56
   The promise of Spiritual Betrothal 59
   Watch out! 60

Mansion 6 65
   Wounded by love 65
   A flame within 66
   Locutions 67
   Rapture 68
   The test of genuine religious experience 70
   Sorrow for sin 71
   Looking at Jesus 72
   About visions 74
   God's chalice 75

Mansion 7 77
   Spiritual Marriage 77
   Darkness and light 78
   Teresa's own experience 79
   Betrothal and marriage compared 80
   The new life in Christ 82
   Bearing trials 83
   The zeal of the saints 84

Postcript 87
For further reading 89

INTRODUCTION

The *Interior Castle*, also known as the *Book of Mansions*, is considered Teresa of Avila's greatest and most mature explanation of the spiritual journey, containing as it does a complete synthesis of her teaching on prayer. The book was written with her nuns in mind. These sisters were neither theologians nor particularly well educated, some indeed were illiterate; but there was little teaching available for women, and the manuscript was initially intended for reading aloud in community.

Teresa began writing in 1577. It was the Feast of the Holy Trinity, June 2nd, when she took up her pen and thought of an image to use, settling on that of a castle with many rooms. At this point she was sixty two years old and was confined to the Carmel of Toledo in disgrace. Her superiors thought she was a 'gadabout' making her foundations in many cities, and they said she must stay within one of her monasteries and remain in enclosure. At every turn she was pressed to defend her reform of the Carmelite Order, keeping up a wide correspondence and attending meanwhile to other business matters. However, she set about the task of writing for her sisters: 'I will be talking to them as I go along,' she wrote, and 'women best understand each other's language.' In other words, she was writing for women she loved and who loved her, so she knew they would listen to what she had to share with them in her inimitable, chatty style.

Half way through the manuscript, Teresa had to discontinue her task in order to travel to Avila on business, and she only took up writing again in November of that year. All in all the book was completed in two halves in a total of six weeks, an incredible feat!

The *Interior Castle* treats of the spiritual journey in a totally original way. Here Teresa is not theorizing from books; instead she writes and speaks from personal experience and close observation of others. It is a psychological rather than a theological work. Instead of a linear progress Teresa uses the image of an open interior space, a space of integration more like a spiral than a straight line. Within the castle's confines she will chart her own development while also stressing that there are other rooms she has not been in. Each reader or listener must adapt her own experience to a general pattern without any slavish imitation.

For Teresa, growing spiritually is travelling inwards to the centre of our being where God dwells, yet too few set out with resolution to reach the Divine Presence. We decide to stop journeying some way along the line and make our home, not in Christ, but in some other place, where we feel comfortable and ready to settle down. Teresa writes to actuate our desire for true fulfilment, making our baptismal grace a reality. We have all received this divine 'seed' at Baptism, but it needs to germinate and grow in order to reach full potential – total transformation in Christ. Only as we progressively surrender ourselves at ever deeper levels are we able to 'become what we were born to be' men and women who are united to God fully and freely.

In this book we have St Teresa's most celebrated images: the castle, the palmito, the hedgehog, the tortoise, the bee, the silkworm, the soul as a wax seal ready to receive God's imprint.

As she writes, her sole aim is, she says, to praise God and lead others to do so too. As always she stresses that prayer and life are interlinked and that writing about prayer must have its parallel influence on daily life. We pray as we live and live as we pray. God and neighbour are inseparable.

General plan of the Interior Castle

The mansions are like staging posts we reach, or rooms we enter, on the way to union with God. They offer a general pattern of growth, even though individuals may vary.

Mansions 1-3 chart the preliminary stages where our own efforts are paramount.

Mansion 4 is a transitional mansion where God begins to take the initiative rather than ourselves.

Mansions 5 and 6 are those where Christ becomes ever more important and we are open to the deepening work of God within us.

Mansion 7 is that of the Spiritual Marriage, the goal of the whole journey, where God is all in all.

Outline of the mansions

In Mansion 1 the soul is introduced as having a natural capacity for God. Here we begin to enter the castle through growing in self-knowledge, prayer and meditation, even if prayer is sporadic and weak. At this early stage sinful behaviour is still in evidence, but if we realise our innate value we will want to activate our true potential to grow and to change. Mansion 2 is the mansion of 'first conversion'. We are touched by God through good reading, sermons, meditating on the truths of faith and so forth. Faults are combated with seriousness. There is a growing love of Christ and others, nature cooperating with grace.

Mansion 3 is the mansion of possible false security because a certain outward level of good behaviour has been reached. It is easy here to judge others unfavourably and trust in our own achievements and goodness. We are 'saints' in our own eyes and look down on others whose outward behaviour is less 'perfect' than our own!

However, if we really want to progress we need humility, non-judgementalness, the ability to examine ourselves on the word 'enough'. If we think we have come 'far enough' then beware! The outward self has been tidied up and looks respectable, but the inner self is weak. There is still far to go.

Mansion 4 is the mansion of transition. Here God begins to take over our lives and our prayer. This usually happens only after a long time spent in the earlier mansions, where human effort is paramount (aided of course by God's grace). At prayer thinking is replaced by loving, often a loving, wordless gaze.

Rather than being turned in upon self the heart is enlarged, and this is a direct gift of God. Sweetness in prayer may come through thinking, but enlargement of heart is not ours to have on demand.

In the fourth mansion the will of God becomes all important. 'What does God want?' is the heart's cry. Whether it be joy or suffering matters not.

Mansion 5 is the beginning of the process of true transformation in Christ, and here Teresa develops her celebrated analogy of the silkworm dying within its cocoon and emerging as a butterfly. This mansion is the mansion of what many call 'second conversion', a deep and radical choice of God. Here we are marked indelibly by God's seal, winging towards the goal of Union. After this a return to earlier mansions is well nigh impossible, but there is a possibility of refusing to go forward as we should.

Teresa says it is as if the contract of betrothal has been drawn up and validated, but the actual betrothal ceremony is still in the future, to be made good when the time is right.

In the sixth mansion God begins to work in us at the the deepest level, so we need plenty of encouragement to keep going and accept the purification entailed. Under the image of fire we understand that God increases the burning pain of desire to be wholly united with Him.

Unlike many spiritual writers, Teresa always looks upon prayer as a relationship, and so, while some might think we are now beyond the human, she stresses that we must never let go of the humanity of Christ our Way. If we are stretching after a nebulous 'God' we will go astray. In Jesus, Mary and the saints we discover what it means to be totally surrendered as well as fully human.

While Teresa devotes space to visions and locutions at this stage she is drawing on her own experience where these abounded. For most of us such phenomena will not be part of the spiritual journey, and they should certainly not be desired for their own sake. As always the true test of progress is love of neighbour and a zeal to serve the Lord in whatever way we can.

Mansion 7 is the summit of the spiritual life – union with God in love in the intimacy of the marriage bond. As transformation in Christ has been effected we can now live by the Spirit in complete self-forgetfulness. While union does not imply sinlessness (we always retain our humanity with its natural imperfections) it does imply the total gift of self, resulting in good works and a desire to praise God and help others to do likewise. Here Martha and Mary work together in complete, harmony. Our humanity is filled to the brim even as our capacity tor God increases. It is as in marriage where, living longer and more lovingly together, a couple can always grow in love and understanding even while enjoying the deep relationship already achieved.

Conclusion

Teresa charts a secure path. It is one anybody can follow, provided there is a growing resolve to give God the whole of oneself, harmonising the love of God and the love of neighbour. The spiritual journey is one of friendship with God and with those we live with. It means standing and living in the truth, whether in prayer or in life. This is the way to maturity and true inner peace.

Teresa kept in her breviary the following bookmark which might be termed a summary of her teaching.

> Let nothing disturb you,
> Let nothing affright you,
> All things pass away;
> God alone remains.
> Patience obtains all things.
> Whoever has God
> Wants for nothing.
> God alone suffices.

'SOLO DIOS BASTA.'

The Interior Castle

PREFACE

I was told by the person who asked me to write this book that the Carmelite nuns, my sisters, need someone to help solve the difficulties they may have in prayer. As women understand each others' language best, and as the sisters love me, I want to explain everything clearly and in a way that can be understood by everyone.

If what I write helps even one person to praise the Lord better then it will have been worth the effort on my part. As all comes from the Lord of mercy, all credit to Him and not myself if I succeed.

MANSION 1

The image of the castle

When I was considering what image to use when I started writing, I began to think of the soul as a castle made of a single diamond of very clear crystal, and in that castle are many rooms.

As we know that our soul is made in the image of God and that God loves to take His delight in us, so we can never have a sufficient understanding of the soul's great dignity and beauty. We need to understand this dignity and not think of ourselves as worthless and good for nothing.

If we consider our bodies only, we are stopping at the castle's exterior walls and will never make our way to the centre. Rather, we need to know who we are and where we come from, and that means journeying inwards and getting a better idea of ourselves and all that God calls us to do and to be.

The castle I am talking about contains many rooms, some above, some below, some at the sides and some in the middle. And at the very centre of the castle God dwells and speaks to us in secret.

To enter this wonderful castle (which is our soul) is to go by the way of prayer, otherwise we will remain all our lives in the outer courts among dangerous reptiles and suchlike animals. Prayer at the beginning stages means thinking about who we are talking to when we pray, using the mind and heart as well as the lips, even though we may pray only occasionally.

Jesus healed a man who had been paralysed for over thirty years (John 5:5). Those who live in such a paralysed state regarding prayer need help or they will never enter the castle. But at least they can try to make a start.

People who are full of preoccupations regarding work, money, careers, and so forth show where their real treasure is, and it isn't God! However, occasionally they may say a few prayers and begin to realise that there is more to life than external things. This way they make a beginning, moving from what is temporary to something deeper and more lasting.

The reality of sin

I want you to consider that this beautiful castle, our soul, standing like a tree of life planted beside the living water that is God, can lose its beauty through sin.

As God is the soul's Sun, He always remains within, but is totally obscured by serious wrongdoing. God never departs from us, but we cannot produce good fruit if we decide to live in darkness and away from the springs of living water.

Sin is as if a thick cloth were to be placed over a crystal. Even though the sun might be shining on it, its brightness would have no effect, no ability to make the jewel sparkle with light.

What a great sadness it is to see so many people remain in darkness, unaware of their great dignity and blind to their failings.

We need to have a holy awe in God's presence and remember that any good we may do comes from God, not ourselves. And we should never treat sin lightly as though it did not matter.

The Palmito

Now we will return to the image of the castle with its many rooms.

Don't imagine these rooms arranged in straight rows, but fix your minds on the centre, the room that is occupied by the King.

The image I think best in this regard is that of the palmito (a shrub common in southern Spain with thick layers of leaves enclosing a succulent edible kernel). All the outer rinds of the palmito need to be taken away in order to get at the succulent centre.

In the same way there are many rooms around the centre of the soul where God dwells as in a sweet kernel.

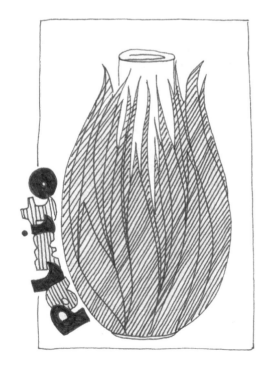

Whenever we think of the soul we should think of it as spacious, ample and lofty, with the Sun that is God reaching every part of it. With such spaciousness and dignity we need the freedom to roam around and explore our inner capacities and not just stop at one room alone.

The bee in the honeycomb

The only room we have to keep coming back to is the room of self knowledge. We must never neglect to grow in the knowledge of self, and that will keep us grounded in humility.

We must be like a bee making honey in the hive, always returning to self-knowledge and humility.

Yet like the bee we must also be ready to fly high and go from flower to flower.

That means taking time to know God and enjoy the good and beautiful things of life, otherwise we may get mired in self-preoccupation and sink into depression – and that helps no one, least of all ourselves.

Let us begin at the beginning, gradually getting to know God and know ourselves, for the two are related.

Knowing God gives us courage to set out on the path that leads to Him, rather than wasting time wondering what others are thinking about us. That's not humility, its pusillanimity!

Walk with your head high, conscious of your dignity and your great calling, not fearful at every obstacle.

Giving time to prayer

There are many ways to enter the castle and many ways to pray. As you get to know yourself you will find the best way for you.

In the early mansions there is not a great deal of light so make the most of what you get. Give God time in whatever way you can.

Proceed with confidence and at a regular pace, rather then trying to do things in fits and starts.

Above all, practice mutual love then you cannot go astray.

And don't go looking for small faults in other people. Keep your eyes on your own – you'll find plenty that need attention!

MANSION 2

Now it is time to think about those people who enter the second mansion, those who have already begun to practice prayer on a regular basis and hear the voice of the Good Shepherd speaking within them. If they cannot do His will immediately at least they are conscious of His call and its sweetness.

How God speaks to us in the second mansion

God doesn't speak with us directly at this point. Rather, God speaks to us through the conversation of good friends, through sermons, through reading good books, and other indirect ways.

Another way God speaks is through the trials and difficulties that we encounter in daily life, or by means of the truths that come to us when we meditate on the things of God when we are at prayer.

What matters is to have great desires and aim high, even though we cannot manage to do as much as we might like. We have just got to be resolute and take no notice of temptations to turn back to an easier life.

Put reason to work and tell yourself that everything is passing and not worth much in the end. After all, death comes to us all at some point, of that we can be sure; and then what will material goods and worldly fame matter?

The prodigal son in a far country was so hungry he was willing to eat pig swill, and yet if he had never left home he could have had all the food he wanted in his father's house. So don't be tempted to wander away from this mansion – you won't find anything worth having elsewhere.

It helps to make friends with people who are living good lives and walking along the same path you wish to travel. That will give you the incentive to keep going.

Be firmly resolved not to give up. The devil doesn't like those who have their minds made up and refuse to budge from the way they think right.

Feelings and favours

I want to make clear that to start praying by looking for all kinds of fine feelings and 'favours' from God is not the way to dig strong and lasting foundations. Feelings come and go and can never be depended upon.

What we must do is prepare ourselves to accept whatever God wants to give us, whether in prayer or in life.

Doing God's will is what counts, not trying to make God do our will. That is a recipe for disaster.

But if we should fall from time to time, don't lose heart. God can bring good out of bad if only we are open to make the most of our mistakes.

True peace

We all want peace, but unless we have peace in our own house it is useless to seek it elsewhere.

Only Christ gives true peace, and that isn't necessarily ease and easy-goingness, though we might like to think so.

Resolve to do the hard things with love. Embrace the Cross. This will enable you to fight with greater resolve and attain the peace won by the blood of Christ.

If necessary seek advice from those more experienced than you are.

And keep your eyes on Jesus. He is the Way to the Father. He is your true friend. He is the companion of your life and your prayer. With Him beside you you cannot go astray.

MANSION 3

Having come thus far you may be tempted to self-satisfaction, but don't rest on your laurels!

It is a great thing to have reached the third mansion, but we are not secure at this stage. We still have to be aware of the enemy at the gates. The only true security is when we reach heaven.

Even some saints fell into grave sin despite having come a long way in God's service. So keep alert and watchful!

We may have Our Lady as patroness of Carmel but that does not guarantee our own holiness. David too was a holy man, and look at what his son Solomon became.

If we are living excellent lives and being faithful to prayer we must always remember the Scripture verse 'Blessed is the one who fears the Lord' (Ps 111:1) and be not over-confident.

Qualities of the third mansion

There are many people in the third mansion who have overcome their initial difficulties:

They avoid even small sins.
They find joy in mortifying themselves.
They spend hours in prayer and recollection.
They use their time well.
They are charitable towards their neighbours.
They fulfil the duties of their state of life conscientiously.

We tend to say that such people are 'saints'.
Well, I say otherwise!

Holiness is far more than an outwardly well ordered life.

Remember the rich young man who was living a good life yet faltered when challenged to sell everything if he wanted to be perfect.

Doing what one has to do anyway is hardly great holiness, and certainly not perfection.

Remember that we are only God's servants and bound to do what is right and good without looking for reward or congratulations from others, never mind congratulating ourselves.

Jesus was a true servant and never looked for compliments or rewards; instead he was focussed on the Cross and on giving his life for us.

If we are expecting God to reward our faithfulness with sweetness in prayer we have the wrong idea of the spiritual life altogether, never mind expecting other people to congratulate us on our good living.

On being tested

The way to discover if we have really advanced is to notice how we react when tested.

Oh my! How some people who seem to be such good Christians go under at even small trials! I have been driven crazy by such people and their constant complaining.

It's no use offering them advice as they think they are far advanced on the spiritual path and know all the answers.

Their only hope is to realise that they are still needy people and not as good as they thought.

It is one thing to meditate on the sufferings of the Lord, but quite another to accept a bit of suffering ourselves. Thinking on the Passion is fine in its own way. Putting the lessons of the Passion into practice in our life is quite another matter.

Loss of reputation makes people in this mansion restless.

They also become depressed over really trifling matters, and if they do manage to rise above trivialities for a time, they think themselves absolutely wonderful. How ridiculous can you get!

If you cannot accept the trials of daily life, stop considering yourself saintly and return to basic humility.

Doing penance

People who have reached the third mansion are quite fond of doing penance but it must be penance of their own choosing. They are so careful about their health that they certainly never go beyond the most basic forms of self denial. This is to move at a snail's pace and think it is alright to do so. There is no sense of challenge, no awareness of the preciousness of life and time.

Why travel so slowly that you take a year to reach your destination when you could do it in a week? Travelling like this is far more exhausting than walking energetically and with a sense of purpose.

Rally yourselves! Keep moving and you will find your energy renewed and your heart strengthened in the process.

Decide that reaching the goal is what matters and stop being put off by every small thing that gets in the way.

Look to your own failings

One of the problems with those who have reached the third mansion is that they tend to criticise others who seem less 'perfect'. They are easily shocked when they might well learn some important things from the people who 'shock' them.

Outward behaviour is not the most important thing, and not everyone is called to travel the same road in the same way. Resist the impulse to put other straight, thinking they should be following the same path as you are.

Learn to keep silent and let others be as they are without criticising them.

MANSION 4

Nearer to the King

This fourth mansion brings us closer to the King who dwells in the centre of the castle.

Usually, though not always, to reach this far we need to have spent quite a long time in the other rooms.

Dangerous creatures hardly ever get into this part of the castle, but if they do they are generally harmless, for the soul is well fortified.

Sweetness in prayer and spiritual consolations

Sweetness in prayer at this stage can have natural roots, like anything that gives us joy: good news, valuable gifts, success in business and so forth.

The kind of sweetness in prayer that gives us joy when we have meditated well has its source in our human nature and is basically human in origin.

On the other hand, genuine spiritual consolations have their source in God even though we may enjoy them in a natural way.

The first kind of spiritual sweetness, springing from our nature, does not enlarge the heart, but it does give us joy in prayer and encourages us to make the effort needed to continue, so it should not be despised.

The most important thing in prayer is not to THINK much but to LOVE much. So when you go to pray do whatever helps you to love the most.

And what does love consist in? It is shown in conforming our will to God's will in all things, praying for God's Kingdom to come, and doing all we can to further the cause of God's church. If we think it is about having no distractions when we pray, or feeling spiritual sweetness, we are mistaken.

Distracting thoughts

Thoughts come and go and we just cannot get hold of them and control them as we would like.

We cannot stop the moon and stars in their course any more than we can stop thinking.

So don't get depressed about this, giving up the struggle. Just keep trying to remain gently in God's presence without forcing yourself to great concentration.

Our human nature is such that at one time we feel one thing, at another time, another.

We need to understand ourselves and remain at peace no matter how we feel or how many distractions we have to cope with.

Don't forget - we are human beings, not angels!

The Prayer of Quiet

Consolations which come from God I term the Prayer of Quiet.

Let me give you an example:

Two large basins can be filled in different ways:

One basin is filled by water that comes from a great distance and through numerous channels.

The other basin is constructed at the very source of the water and fills without any noise or effort.

The water that comes by way of channels is like the water that comes through meditation. It engages our thoughts and means we have to make an effort and be interiorly busy.

The fountain of water coming direct from the source is accompanied by great peace and quietness.

It gives us a happiness that does not seem to originate on earth but in a much deeper part of the soul.

The test of genuine prayer that comes from God is that it increases our humility.

That is why consolations in prayer should not be sought.

We need to love God without wanting anything for self and, as God is supreme Master, we must allow Him to give and take as He chooses and not according to our own miserable standards.

The Prayer of Recollection

In this prayer we find ourselves building a kind of temple within, where exterior things gradually lose their hold over us. It is as if the soul enters within itself or rises above itself.

Here we gradually learn to listen to the voice of the Good Shepherd and leave distractions and sins aside. We begin to realise that God truly dwells within us and we want to find Him there.

When we are in the stage of the Prayer of Recollection

there is an enlargement of heart, enabling us to contain the water running into the basin of our soul from the fountain of God.

This enlargement of heart makes interior space within us, giving courage for action and a great desire to serve and love the Lord, even at cost to the self.

There is a growing understanding that only God matters and a desire to please Him alone.

We recognise that we are gradually being drawn inwards by God, like a tortoise or a hedgehog retiring into its shell. But this simile is not exact because these animals can decide to hide themselves in themselves at will, whereas with us it only happens when God pleases. This is a grace granted to those who are already leaving the world behind.

When I say 'leaving the world' I am not talking about being a monk or a nun. A married person too can leave the world in the sense I am talking about. It's to do with giving God absolute freedom to act within us.

Praise God if you are thus far in your spiritual journey, and try to put your reasoning powers on one side so as to discover what God is doing in the secret part of your soul.

Awakening love

At prayer try to be silent and just stay near the Lord.

But if this is not happening don't just sit about like an empty headed ninny. Put the understanding to work and do whatever you can to increase your love of God - meditation, service of others, intercession, works of charity, penance and so forth.

Don't try to over-exert yourself, straining to become 'quiet'. Leave yourself in God's hands, disregarding your own advantage and practising self-forgetfulness.

in God's hands

49

Two warnings

If you have come this far I entreat you to take every care to keep from any kind of sin, because you are not yet sufficiently strong to resist temptation.

People at this stage are like babies at the breast, and we know that a baby taken from its mother will die.

To give in to the temptation to stop praying at this stage is seriously wrong. God has led you thus far. God is wanting to give Himself completely to you, and then you turn away.

Never have such confidence in yourself that you abandon the search for God and God's will, because the Enemy will do everything possible to make you turn back, knowing that one person given wholly to the Lord will attract many others.

On the other hand I must address those who suffer from fragile physical or psychic health, for if we have weak health and weaken ourselves further by prolonged prayer and penance we might think that to abandon themselves to absorption in God is to make progress. Living in the 'airy fairy' is not holiness or anything like it.

We persuade ourselves that our weakened state is God-given rapture, whereas it is merely self-induced foolishness that further injures our health.

A person like this is cured of such foolishness by being told to eat more, sleep more, and not take herself so seriously.

Languishing around is actually lazing around and gets you nowhere.

If this weakness persists realise that God calls you to an active life which keeps your feet firmly on the ground, not among the clouds. A community needs all sorts, but can do without those who try to live lives that are not in step with their particular temperament.

So discover your strengths and weaknesses and live accordingly.

Common sense could do with being more common.

MANSION 5

If we want to make real progress in this mansion then it is important to keep absolutely nothing back from God, whether it be little or much. Such strong resolution means the devil cannot get into us at this stage, we have become focused upon God in reality and not merely in the imagination. This is the path of wisdom rather than knowledge, of direct contact with God as God is, even though the period of direct contact may be short.

In this mansion the Lord brings us into the 'wine cellar of the king' (cf Song of Songs 3:2). It is like the Lord entering the Upper Room where the disciples were staying after the Resurrection. He came through closed doors to wish them peace and they did not know how He entered. He was just there, as He was when He left the tomb on Easter Day.

The analogy of the silkworm

You will have heard of the wonderful way in which silk is made. When a mulberry tree begins to come into leaf the silkworm, no bigger than a tiny seed, begins to develop. It then starts to feed on the mulberry leaves until it is a full grown worm, when it begins to spin itself into a tight cocoon of silk. Finally, the worm, which was large and ugly, emerges as a beautiful white butterfly.

This story might seem unbelievable, but it is true. The worm loses its wormlike life and becomes a free and beautiful thing, quite unlike its initial being.

This is an image of the soul which, through the inspiration of the Holy Spirit, begins to make use of the general help God gives to us all – frequent confession, good books, devoted friends who love God, meditation on the truths of faith, and so forth. The soul then nourishes itself on this food and becomes strong.

When it is fully grown the soul begins to spin its cocoon like a house in which it is to die. It is like hiding oneself in God, dying to self, and emerging reborn in the very life of Christ.

So let us begin to spin this cocoon, renouncing self-love and self-aggrandisement, practising prayer, penance, obedience and all the good works that we know of. In this way we die to self and begin to live in Christ. In prayer we prepare to become, as it were, that beautiful white butterfly, free and unfettered.

Another image would be to compare ourselves to the dove Noah released from the ark. It looked for some resting place on the flood waters but found none.

Once we have tasted God in freedom we cannot easily settle anywhere until we experience once again the beauty of union with Him. With wings to fly we want to do everything God asks, and do it willingly and promptly.
Surely now we cannot go back to where we came from, just as a butterfly cannot return to its wormlike existence. But we can find no rest until God gives us the peace of the Divine presence permanently, and that is not yet possible. There will be suffering and trials of all kinds before this happens.

The soul as a wax seal

Without knowing how it happens a soul in this state is like soft wax upon which God can place His seal. The wax has only to be there, softened and ready, consenting to accept the imprint of God upon it.

Surely this is the greatest gift God could give us, a sign that we belong completely to Him – marked with His seal forever.

Never, I think, will God grant this favour unless He has determined to have us for His very own.

The importance of loving others

We may have come a long way in God's service but we always have to be vigilant and not just trust in ourselves and our experience in prayer. Self love, judgemental attitudes, failures in love, can gnaw through our supposed 'virtues' like the worm that gnawed through Jonas's ivy (Jonas 4:6-7).

Things happen to us and we have to 'make a virtue of necessity' as they say, even when we cannot do as well as we might like.

The most important thing of all is love of God and love of our neighbour. These are the virtues we must strive for.

The surest sign that we are growing in the love of God is that we should be really loving our neighbour. We may think we are loving God but the only real proof is our love for others. As this pleases God the most, God will be sure to grant us a greater love for Him also in the process, for love of God and love of neighbour have one and the same root – God.

We may think when we are at prayer that we are progressing well, considering meanwhile all the fine things we will do to spread the love of God around. But our actions will soon show whether or not our prayer is genuine.

It's not just about playing a good tune but having our actions in harmony with the music we play!

I really have to laugh at some people who get all psyched up about their prayer, trying to hold on to good feelings and such like, as if they could reach God if only they concentrated hard enough! What God desires isn't feelings but works.

God wants us to live humbly in the truth of who we are, so be glad to hear others praised.

Try to accept self-knowledge even when it is painful.

Keep silent. Eschew gossip. Take on yourselves the diminishment that comes with hard work while others have leisure. These are the things that matter.

Consider Jesus who died for you on the Cross. This will enable you to stop complaining and take life bravely and generously on board.

Don't make yourself the centre of the universe. Put God there and you will be happy.

The promise of Spiritual Betrothal

I liken prayer at this stage to people who are on the brink of getting engaged.

They discuss whether or not they are suited to one another and whether they really love each other enough for a lifetime commitment.

They continue to meet and to get to know one another better so that an engagement can be entered into with clarity, and a desire to marry in due course.

It is like this in the spiritual life. A contract of betrothal has been drawn up and the soul begins to understand what a blessed future awaits her. So she is determined to do the will of her divine Spouse in every way that can give Him pleasure.

This engenders a sense of longing. But it can be dissipated if the soul becomes neglectful and sets her affection on other things or persons in the meantime.

So, I just want to warn you to watch out for ways in which sin can enter in and spoil what has been achieved.

Watch out!

I have personally known people get so far and then turn back under great temptation. Be careful and don't trust in yourself! Look at the example of people like Saint Dominic, St Francis, Ignatius of Loyola and others. One holy person leads many others to God. They give us examples of people who were faithful to graces received.

If we follow the will of God carefully, as they did, then obviously we will not be lost. But what happens is that faults creep in little by little if we are not vigilant.

There is no enclosure so secure, no desert so remote, that we can let down our guard.

We need to be very careful to ask God in prayer to keep us in His hands, and remember that if God leaves us even for a moment we shall fall.

Most of all we must see whether or not we are advancing in virtue. Are we growing in kindness, honesty, humility, love of others? And if we are not advancing we must cherish misgivings.

Real love is always active.

If you want to be the bride of the Lord and have come this far you must not lie down as if all is already accomplished. Far from it! Fix your eyes on God and the journey ahead. The goal is still distant.

MANSION 6

Wounded by love

In this mansion the soul has been wounded with love of her Spouse and seeks opportunities for solitude, for being alone with God, in a way that shows her deep desire to have no other joy but Him.

This is not accomplished without great trials, sometimes inner sufferings and sometimes bodily sickness. But the soul has grown stronger and is ready to bear whatever comes.

We can't see ahead, thank God, or we might repine if we knew the future beforehand!

One of the problems is that people who are close to God can be taunted about how holy they seem to be getting; how their life is a sham; how people can be good Christians without going to these extremes! Then they are told of how someone else ruined her life and dragged others down with her through being too pious.

I know this from my own experience! Some people liked me, but many others gave me a wide berth!

However, at this stage we want only the honour and glory of God, not our own honour, and so we brush off these criticisms and praise God for whatever comes our way.

Leave all care about your reputation in God's hands. Don't live by what others think of you – its a waste of time and effort to be always on the lookout for opportunities to please people and to be afraid of censure. It does the truth no good. Be simple, open, straightforward in all your dealings, and leave the rest to the Lord.

A flame within

There is a growing understanding that God is with the soul at this stage, and a consciousness of God's presence.

It is as if a burning brazier were giving out showers of sparks. We feel the heat but are not burned up by it. Far from being numbed, all our faculties and senses are alert and active. This burning love which has begun to consume us is a great grace and blessing. If we have received even a tiny spark it should fill us with joy and a desire to give God all we can.

This grace is one that cannot be duplicated by the devil or manufactured by the imagination. It comes straight from the Lord.

Locutions

Another way God awakens us may be by means of words heard interiorly, but this demands great discernment lest words just proceed from our imagination.

Depression can be a factor here so just be on the alert. Someone else may see the way more clearly than we do ourselves, so ask advice from experienced guides.

Be aware that inner locutions do not make us any better than others who hear nothing but live good lives.

Words that really come from God engender humility, courage in action and tranquil trust in adversity. They remain with us and are proved by the fruit they bear.

Real words from God are heard intellectually deep in the soul, beyond all feeling and understanding. It is impossible to ignore them.

Rapture

In rapture the fire of love within begins to send out more sparks to enkindle love. The Lord is then able to reveal more of His mysteries to us.

Remember Moses and the burning bush, (cf Ex 3:2) Moses could not describe everything he saw, only what God revealed and secretly explained. Yet even with partial knowledge Moses became aware of the truth of God's being and was strengthened to lead the Israelites to freedom. Amid the thorns of the burning bush he must have learned many things. He was empowered to act even without full understanding of God's greatness and glory.

Rapture is real. It gives us power to act. It puts us in touch with the great glory and goodness of God even when we cannot describe or understand it fully.

When you enter a private apartment of some great lord you will see all kinds of ornaments and glassware, too many to be used in daily life. In fact, with such a variety of things on display it is impossible to remember them all individually. It is the same in rapture. Individual things fade before the impress of the whole. It is as if the doors of the castle were shut in order to have quiet communion with the Bridegroom. It may be only for a short time but the joy is 'out of this world'.

Another form of rapture I call a 'flight of the spirit' when the soul seems to be transported into God, like a great wave lifting a little ship.

Once I myself was looking at a Crucifix and thinking I had nothing to offer God, when Jesus comforted me by saying I could offer His pains to the Father. This experience I have never forgotten.

The test of genuine religious experience

At this stage there is a tension between the desire to spend time alone with God and the desire to do everything possible to further God's cause in the world by loving action, helping others to praise God more.

The little butterfly seems both free and bound – free to praise God, bound by ties that keep her fettered to the world and its many demands.

What is certain is that self-interest dissolves and the mercy of God comes to the forefront. With St Martin we must say 'Lord, if I am still necessary to your people, I do not refuse to labour for them. Your will be done'. (Office of St Martin of Tours)

Tears of love and desire may be deceptive. They can be self-induced for one thing. Real tears from God water the ground of the soul and produce the fruit of good works, rather than a maudlin outlook on life.

Closeness to God brings peace and happiness no matter what else is going on in our life.

Look at St Francis who told robbers who accosted him

that he was the 'Herald of the great King'. Some might think him mad, but he certainly knew how to praise God in adversity!

Praise God all of you, and arouse others to praise God too. Praise is catching. Spread it around!

Sorrow for sin

The more we know God and ourselves the more we will understand our sinful condition. This has nothing to do with the fear of hell, indeed that is not present at all in the sixth mansion.

Instead there is a holy fear, a sense of not being all we could or should be when we have received so much love and kindness.

true sorrow

Looking at Jesus

We must never let go of our Lord's humanity, continually meditating on the life and Passion of Jesus, and that of the Virgin and other saints. Jesus is our guide, and without Him we will never find the way to the Father. Jesus Himself said 'I am the Way' (Jn 14:6) so don't ever seek to depart from His presence.

We have to use our minds and imagination if need be and not just rely on passing inspiration. A firm foundation is necessary and we find it in meditating on the life of Christ. The more we meditate the deeper will our understanding and appreciation of our faith grow. Looking at Christ is looking at God, and we grow like what we see and live with.

The company of our good Jesus, the Blessed Virgin and the saints is too good to ignore, and it keeps us grounded.

The little bird, the little butterfly, can easily flit around in the air without realising it must rest upon the person of Jesus and not go seeking for something else that is more elusive.

About visions

I have seen a number of visions, but the real test as always is how we live our life.

Visions can be intellectual or imaginary; but they are gifts of God and can never be demanded as of right, nor can they be 'deserved'. God is free and we must let God be God and not seek anything out of the ordinary.

Humility is the virtue we need most. Why?

I discovered the answer when I was thinking about this and it dawned on me that humility is the truth, and to be humble is to walk in truth before God and others, and not wish to be thought better than we are. Anyone who doesn't understand this walks in falsehood.

Knowing ourselves keeps us humble and truthful in word and deed, whereas 'visions' can be illusory.

God's chalice

Those who advance on the road of prayer and life are ready for everything.

Jesus asked his disciples whether they could drink from his chalice and they said 'We can' (cf Matt 20:22).

We should be able to say the same, and be ready to accept any suffering that comes our way.

God will speak up for us if necessary – as He did for Mary Magdalene – and in the end repay all our suffering with good.

MANSION 7

Spiritual Marriage

What I have said is only a fraction of all God will do for us in His mercy. May He now guide my pen as I start to talk to you about the seventh mansion which is the mansion of those He has taken to be His brides.

Just as God dwells in heaven, so He needs a place to dwell upon earth as in a second heaven; and here He dwells in people who have withheld nothing from Him.

For those brought to the Spiritual Marriage, through the Prayer of Union, God makes them able to see and understand something of the favour they are now receiving. They are so closely united to the Bridegroom that wherever they are and whatever they do He is with them. Even though they may not feel anything in their senses they have an obscure intuition that they are always with the Lord and alive in the mystery of the Trinity.

You may think that someone in this state is living more in heaven than on earth, absorbed in God's presence, but this is not so at all. Someone like this is more alert than ever in God's service, although when not actually working she rests in God's happy companionship.

And she certainly never forgets to pray for those in need, that they too may be fed with heavenly food. Intercessory prayer is powerful in its outreach.

Darkness and light

At this stage we are like a person who is with others in a very brightly lit room.

However, when the shutters are closed everything is in darkness, and we are unable to see anything or anyone until the shutters are once more opened.

Opening the shutters depends on the Lord's mercy, for seeing the light is not in our own power.

In the same way, a conscious experience of God's presence depends on having light, though we can be intuitively aware that God is present even in darkness when the shutters are closed.

We just know that God is there by faith, not sight, and are certain we are never absent from Him.

Teresa's own experience

The Lord reveals the Divine Presence in different ways to different people. I saw Him one day after Communion, where He appeared in great beauty and majesty as He did after the Resurrection. He told me that it was time that I took His affairs upon myself while He would take on mine. He said more, which I understood but cannot easily repeat.

I knew that the Lord had spoken to me before, but this was of a quite different quality. It is like the difference between those who are merely betrothed and those who are one in the bond of marriage. This union is not bodily but takes place in the deepest centre of the soul, bringing peace as Jesus brought peace to the apostles when He entered through closed doors after the Resurrection.

Betrothal and marriage compared

In the period of Spiritual Betrothal which is the sixth mansion the two concerned, God and ourselves, can be separated. We may be united in heart and soul, but often we are apart and remain two distinct individuals. The soul can be deprived of the Lord's companionship at this point, at least as far as the understanding goes.

It is like two wax tapers which can be joined to make one flame, yet they are still two, and can be separated to burn alone or together.

In the Spiritual Marriage the analogy is not of two conjoined candles but of rain falling from heaven into a river or spring. Here in the water nothing can be separated.

It is like a tiny streamlet entering the sea and becoming one with it, or like two large windows letting light into a room and becoming one light. As St Paul says, 'For me to live is Christ and to die is gain' (Phil 1:21). The little butterfly I have spoken of has now died and only Christ is its life.

No matter what happens to us in daily life, we are constantly aware of the greatness of God and God's presence in the midst of the soul, like a great river or a consuming fire with which we are one.

A soul in this state remains humble and does not trust in itself. Instead it is always on the lookout for ways to serve God better and with greater love, avoiding even the smallest sin.

The new life in Christ

Let us look at the life of this little butterfly who has died to itself and risen to life in Christ, and the effects we can notice in her.

First, a complete self-forgetfulness.

Second, total abandonment to God's will, whether suffering is involved or not.

Third, a tender love for the Lord no matter what happens, and a desire to see God loved by all.

Fourth, great inner tranquillity and peace in all circumstances.

Sometimes there may be temptations and inner turmoil, but the Lord gives the soul great determination and resolution not to give in, and so it grows stronger all the time.

Don't think these people are already perfect, that is sinless and without any imperfections. This is not so at all. We remain frail human beings, not angels!

Jesus Himself was tempted, so we cannot expect that all will be easy and plain sailing.

Bearing trials

We always find that those who walked closely with Christ had to bear many trials.

Look at His Mother and the apostles.

Consider St Paul who had visions yet never stopped working really hard to please God and spread the Gospel throughout the world.

I like the story of St Peter fleeing from Rome. He met the Lord on the road and went straight back to his death. And fortunately the Lord provided someone to kill him.

My sisters, how little we should think about resting, being honoured, esteemed and so forth, when God wants to live within us! Rather, we will always be thinking of ways to please Him and show our love. This is the end of the Spiritual Marriage which always gives birth to good works.

Fix your eyes on the Crucified Lord and all will seem easy. When you see Christ's suffering how can you imagine we can please Him simply be saying certain words. Instead we have to be branded with the sign of the cross and become slaves of God.

The foundation of this building is humility. Any other foundation will bring your castle tumbling down around your ears!

I repeat. Don't try and build on prayer and contemplation alone. Look to your actions and to how you practice the virtues or you will remain stunted. And God grant nothing worse may happen, for whoever does not advance on the spiritual path soon begins to go backwards.

In prayer we gain the strength needed for service, not for daydreaming and enjoying ourselves.

The zeal of the saints

Look at the prophet Elijah, St Francis and St Dominic, St Mary Magdalen and others. They were truly zealous in bringing souls to God even at cost to themselves.

Martha and Mary must work together. Work alone or prayer alone is not enough – we need both.

If we cannot go out to the mission fields there are always people close by who we can bring to God. We cannot help everyone, but we can help those we live with and who we meet in our daily life and work. So don't go making grand plans that will never materialise.

See what is at hand and do it.

God does not look so much at the greatness of our works as at the love with which we do what has to be done here and now.

May it please God that in this way we will live lives of sacrifice and praise. And may God grant that I may live as I have described here, through the merits of His Son, who lives and reigns forever. Amen.

Path of Prayer

POSTSCRIPT

I began to write this book with some reluctance, but now I am glad that I made the necessary effort.

You can enter and walk about in this castle wherever you are, and do so freely without seeking anyone's permission.

It is not a matter here of deciding ourselves which mansions we will enter; but at least we can make a start, and hopefully in time we will reach the centre.

I have written here only of seven mansions but there are many more to explore – above, below, gardens, fountains, all kinds of things to help you know and love God better.

I submit all I have written to Holy Church in which I wish to live and die.

May God be praised for ever. Amen. Amen.

FOR FURTHER READING

Texts

Billy D., *Interior Castle with Commentary*, Ave Maria
    Press, 2007
Rodriguez O. & Kavanagh K. (Trans), *Teresa of Avila,
    Complete Works*, ICS Publications, 1980
Backhouse H.(ed), *Teresa of Avila, Interior Castle*, Hodder
    & Stoughton, 1988
E Allison Peers (Trans), *Teresa of Avila, Complete Works*,
    Sheed & Ward. 1972

General

Ashbrook R.T., *Mansions of the Heart*, Jossey-Bass, 2009
Bourne P., *St Teresa's Castle of the Soul*, Wenzel Press, 1995
Burney CM., *God Alone is Enough*, Paraclete Press, 1964
Burrows R., *Interior Castle Explored*, Sheed & Ward, 1981
Byrne L., T*he Life & Wisdom of Teresa of Avila*, Hodder &
    Stoughton, 1988
Don M., *Falling into the Arms of God*, New World Library,
    2005
Dubay T., *Fire Within*, Ignatius Press, 1989
Green D., *Gold in the Crucible*, Element Books, 1989
Gross F.L., *The Making of a Mystic*, State University of New York
    Press, 1993
McLean J., *Towards Mystical Union*, St Pauls, 2003

Other Titles in the Series 'For Everyone':

A Taste of Hildegard
ISBN: 978-1-905039-17-3

Life in God's Now
ISBN: 978-1-905039-11-1

St Teresa's Way of Perfection for Everyone
ISBN: 0-904287-78-5

The Living Flame of Love
ISBN: 0-904287-88-2

Introducing Julian, Woman of Norwich
ISBN: 9781905039142

Gospel Childhood
ISBN: 0-904287-94-7

The Cloud Of Unknowing For Everyone
ISBN: 978-0-904287-97-4

Our Fr St Benedict
ISBN: 978-1-905039-06-7